Darkness, light and everything inbetween.

Amy Claire Atkinson

BookLeaf
Publishing

Presentation by *BookLeaf Publishing*

Web: www.bookleafpub.com

E-mail: info@bookleafpub.com

ISBN: 9789357619189

First edition 2023

Dedicated to my beautiful daughter Isla & the love of my life, Joel. They are my world, my reason.

PREFACE

Becoming a mother changed my life, my heart beat not just for me but for another little life outside of my body. It made me more vulnerable, stressed but ultimately happier than ever before. Nearly losing my husband to cancer showed me the fragility of life but filled us all with the burning desire to live. To fight through the hard times and let love win. This poetry book takes you on our journey, battling cancer as a family and finding beauty in all life's little moments.

The darkness.

What lies beneath your skin?
Buried deep within
everyday living becomes a task,
searching for answers,
screaming for help behind our masks.

In a haze of panic,
they deliver us the answer,
after waiting all this time
the word we never want to hear
'cancer'
we are paralysed by fear.

Eyes widen. Hands grip.
Into the cancer pathway we slip
blindly trying to navigate the unknown
I leave you at the hospital
and return to our family home.

Too young to walk these corridors
too young to face this fight
but fate has dealt us this hand
and I will steer you towards the light.

A Letter to my daughter

You will always be my little girl.
My darling daughter you shall always be.
Even when you're too grown up to sit upon my knee
and you realise that not every story has a happily ever after,
I'll be there to hold your hand,
and turn your tears to laughter.

You'll always be my little girl;
The one too shy to look strangers in the eye.
The one who ran through fields of daisies
and picked me the biggest one.
The one who made me so proud.
The one who made me a mum.

You'll always be my little girl
and as I watch you grow
I hope the world is kind to you
and I hope you'll always know
that my home is your home
my love is yours always
and everything will be alright if we are kind and brave

The Relentless Night.

You are the stars in my sky
pushing through the darkness
reminding me of the light.
The beauty amid the fear of the relentless night.
A constant breathtaking reminder
that everything will be alright.

Cancer.

Nothing is promised in this life,
be grateful for what you've got.
Sometimes you've got to roll with the punches,
count your blessings
because despite everything we still have a lot.

Give me a walk around the same old streets holding
your hand,
Give me a night in front of the tv,
Give me a kiss and a cup of tea,
Give me a life full of beautiful simplicity,
full of you and me.

We won't wake in fear of cancer too scared to speak
it's name,
We will say it's name loud and clear
And know that I'm walking every step with you,
I am always here.

We will beat this cancer,
We won't cry or cower,
We will face this storm together,
because with love we have power.

Ventilator.

I reached out to touch you,
you were ice.
My hands retreat.
Our embrace once warm and safe,
now a stranger with a frozen face.
But I know your soul is alive inside.
I feel your heartbeat,
you're silent but alive.
Everyday I sit by your side,
until one day your breath is your own once more.
Out of the battle you walk,
a winner of your own internal war.

Escape

I want to walk until I run out of road;
to a place where the grass meets the skies.
I want to scream until I run out of sound
to escape to a place where I cannot be found.

To a place where I can be at peace with the world
and let the quiet fill my head,
have a moment just me and the blue skies,
picture your hand in mine, stare into your eyes.

With all that I am I wish and I pray
for all your pain to go away.
Everything I own means nothing, all I feel is this space,
the other half of me that cannot be replaced.

The world seems cruel and cold and harsh.
But I know like everything, this hurt will pass
and you'll be back where you belong.
How dare I feel weak? When you are so strong.

So, I'll stand tall for you
I'll rise like the sun
I'll breathe in and out
Because you can beat this,
and of that I have no doubt.

Belief

Keep going,
reaching out for better days.
When you're free falling
through the depth of despair
let other's comforting words be there.
Let them lift us high.
Running towards the light.
Fill every fibre of us with hope & fight,
push through the pain and never lose sight.
Hold tightly onto life.

Fire.

Something exists deep down inside,
A fire.
A pure desire to stay alive.
Fight or flight.
It comes alight.
When all else fades,
hope stays
and we rise like the sun's golden rays.

Fire.

Treading water.

I won't join you in the depths of your despair
because what good would that do?
other than drag you down further,
drowning with you.

Instead,
take my hand.
I will lead you towards the light.
Let's tread water
through these long days & nights.

Until you're ready to swim,
ride the ways,
towards happier days.
We will rise together.
Breathe deep.
It's you and me, forever.

Change

I want to be that girl,
starting out on her journey
full of ambition and energy
hope and determination,
fearless.

When I look in the mirror
I see eyes with shadows
a mouth that has lost its smile
my reflection is a stranger.

And yet, beneath it all
my soul is still searching,
despite all the despair
for a glimmer of light
a flicker of faith.

Because where there is hope,
there is life,
there is light,
there is air.

Scars

We are not broken
We are not beaten
We wear our scars with pride
I am stronger with you by my side.

Scars are the footprints of trauma,
imprinted on your skin,
burned into my memory.
With every beat of my heart
I remember how fragile life is,
how precious everyday is,
how everything can change in a second.

There are days where the past weighs me down
where I carry it around.
There are days where
without you I would have drown.

Fight.

Life can sometimes seem constantly uphill.
Climbing a never-ending mountain, losing the will.
Looking up into the clouds, your goal can seem so far away
Easier to give up, harder to stay.

But it is in these times when the road is steep
that we mustn't quit, we must all dig deep.
For the views that wait when we reach the top
are motivation to keep going, please don't stop.

Life is tough, but you are tougher
The road ahead is unexpected and rougher
than you or I could have ever known
But I know we will find our way back home.

Together we can make it to the top,
take in the views, pause and stop.
Life will be more beautiful because we have learnt along
the way
how fragile it is, and how much we want to stay.

Don't give up, don't you ever quit.
When you get knocked down, when you're hardest hit
look for me and I'll help you find your way,
we will live for tomorrow and fight for today.

Silver lining.

13

The lows are as intense as the highs,
everything seems magnified,
the intensity of life;
when you are in fight or flight.

But you got through yesterday,
you deserve tomorrow.
Feel my love as well as your sorrow.
Every cloud has a silver lining,
so, when life gets tough,
keep on shining.

Spring

We will rise like the flowers of spring.
Nature's reminder
that we made it through
the cold, dark days
and the world is still full of
beauty and light.

Summer

The simplicity of summer's haze.
Happiness found in new places, holidays.
Sipping a cold lemonade
watching the light fade.
A burnt orange sunset.
Fresh cut flowers,
your smile,
the sound of the sea,
you and me.

Our Autumn

Muddy boots,
endless walks,
golden trees and
Therapeutic talks.
Restored by nature,
fueled by hope,

we move under
clear blue skies
trying to disguise
tear-stained eyes.
Put on a happier mask
and wait for this nightmare
to dissolve into our past.

Our winter.

17

The ground is not steady beneath my feet,
stability turned to fragility.
Faith shaken; moments taken.
But hope remains &
we will awaken
to new beginnings
on steadier ground
our faith restored and
happiness found.

My always, My forvever.

I do. I choose you,
not just today, but always.
Our love is infinite, it knows no end,
my soulmate, my love, my best friend.

The promises we made won't ever fade,
I'll walk through life by your side
for the rest of my days,
I will love you forever, always.

Bride for a day, your wife for life.
All of our battles, our troubles and strife
melt away. When I look into your eyes it's all okay,
It's you and me, always.

My flower girl

19

You made me a mum, you changed my life,
you walked by my side as I became a wife.
My beautiful girl, my darling child,
with the sweetest soul and a spirit wild,
when days were dark you got me through,
my sunshine, my reason, my motivation;
it's always you.

New Priorities.

So what if bedtime is a little later?
So what if the washing isn't done?
we will tidy away those worries
and make room for having fun.

Making memories, family time
is what life is all about.
The housework can wait for tomorrow
for now, let's all go out!

Take that trip, explore and venture.
You won't remember the bills and stress
when you're grey and old.
You'll remember, the laughs, the love, the togetherness.

The darkness, light and everything inbetween.

Dark and light,
the constant fight,
sunset, sunrise,
this life is a gift,
this life is ours.

Storms always pass and nights always end,
luck can change and paths can bend.
We are all freefalling at the mercy
of fate's storming.

The future is full of love and light,
let's keep moving towards that.
We won't be living in the shadows forever,
we can get through anything together.

www.ingramcontent.com/pod-product-compliance
Lightning Source LLC
La Vergne TN
LVHW021348200726
843509LV00014B/2723